THE KREGEL PICTORIAL GU[IDE]

EVERYDAY LIFE IN BIBLE TIMES

TIM DOWLEY

kregel
PUBLICATIONS

Grand Rapids, MI 49501

The Kregel Pictorial Guide to Everyday Life in Bible Times by Tim Dowley

Copyright 1998 by Three's Company/Angus Hudson Ltd.

Published in 1999 by Kregel Publications, a division of Kregel, Inc., P.O. Box 2607, Grand Rapids, MI 49501. Kregel Publications provides trusted, biblical publications for Christian growth and service. Your comments and suggestions are valued.

For more information about Kregel Publications, visit our web site at: http://www.kregel.com

Designed by Peter Wyart,
Three's Company
5 Dryden Street
London WC2E 9NW

Picture acknowledgements
All illustrations by Alan Parry, except as follows:
Frank Barber: p. 16 (top); Jeremy Gower: p. 5 (top right); Richard Scott: p. 12 (top right), p. 28.

Photographs
Tim Dowley: pp. 6, 20, 28; Unique Image: p. 18; Peter Wyart: p. 32.

ISBN 0-8254-2465-8

1 2 3 4 5 / 03 02 01 00 99
Printed in Singapore

Also by Kregel Publications

Josephus: The Essential Works
Translated and condensed by Paul L. Maier

An indispensable aid to the study of first-century history—a full-color edition of the essential works of Josephus, newly translated by an internationally known writer and scholar. Key features include: 83 full-color photographs of historic sites and ancient artifacts; 17 maps, charts, and illustrations; and 19 insightful commentaries.

0-8254-3260-x   416 pp.   hardcover

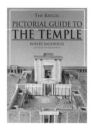

The Kregel Pictorial Guide to the Temple
Robert Backhouse

This fully illustrated resource follows the history of Jewish worship from its early days in the Tent of Meeting at Mount Sinai to the first temple building constructed by Solomon. The enlargement of the second temple building by Herod and the subsequent history of the Temple Mount through the modern era are also covered in fascinating detail.

0-8254-3039-9   32 pp.   paperback

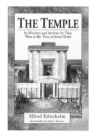

The Temple: Its Ministry and Services As They Were at the Time of Jesus Christ
Alfred Edersheim

The new standard edition of Edersheim! Over 70 full-color illustrations, photographs, maps, and charts. Includes exclusive photographs of Alec Garrard's scale model of the temple. Foreword by British scholar John Bimson provides updated information from recent archaeological findings.

0-8254-2509-3   256 pp.   hardcover

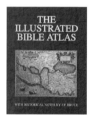

The Illustrated Bible Atlas
F. F. Bruce, CARTA

From the premier producer of biblical and Near Eastern maps, this compact atlas of the Bible covers the history of Israel and the ancient Near East from the second millennium B.C. through the modern era. Each map is accompanied by insightful text by renowned biblical scholar F. F. Bruce.

0-8254-2086-5   32 pp.   paperback

The River Jordan: An Illustrated Guide from Bible Days to the Present
CARTA

This full-color book takes the reader the length of Israel—from the majestic headwaters of the Jordan to the dismal depths of the Dead Sea.

0-8254-2376-7   48 pp.   paperback

PUBLICATIONS | *Challenging minds . . . encouraging hearts*

Available at your local Christian bookstore or by calling 800-733-2607

Contents

Clothing

Men's clothes

Most Jewish men wore an inner garment, an outer garment and sandals. Unlike people today, they were not much influenced by fashion and their dress did not change for centuries. Arabs today often wear similar clothes, because they are best suited to the hot climate of their lands in the Middle East.

The tunic

The inner garment, often called a tunic, was like a close-fitting shirt. It was made of wool, linen or cotton. Some tunics just had slits for the arms; others had long sleeves. Sometimes men wore an undergarment called a loincloth beneath the tunic.

The tunic was often held in at the waist by a belt made of leather or cloth. Sometimes the belt had a pouch to keep money in (Mark 6:8). When a man needed to free himself for hard work, he tucked up his tunic into his belt.

In Bible times people had no special nightclothes. At night they simply loosened their belts and lay down in their tunics.

The cloak

Jewish men wore an outer garment called a cloak or robe. This cloak was made of woollen cloth and was wrapped round the body to help keep warm. It had slits for the arms. At night people used their cloaks as bedcovers.

Rich men often had cloaks made of expensive silk or linen, and with wide sleeves and blue fringes (Matthew 23:5).

Jewellery

Jewish men wore various sorts of jewels and decorations. They often wore a ring on the finger, or on a cord around the neck.

These rings were sometimes used to press into wax on important letters. Each ring made a special mark, called a seal, to show who the letter came from.

Some people also wore magic charms, believing that they would keep away evil spirits.

Hair-styles

Jewish men cut their hair with scissors and long-bladed razors. Sometimes they made special religious vows, and did not cut their hair for a long time. Men often wore skull-caps, with bands of cloth round the edge.

Below centre: the costume of a Jewish man;

below left: Men often hitched their tunic up when they were working in the fields;

below right: Costume of a wealthy Eastern man. Notice his richly-coloured clothing.

Women's Clothes

In Bible times, women wore similar clothes to men.

The tunic

Like the men, women wore a tunic of wool, cotton or linen. But women's tunics were usually worn right down to the ankles, and were often blue in colour. Women's tunics also had V-necks, with embroidery along the edges. Like the men, women lifted the hem of their tunics when they were doing heavy work, such as carrying water.

The woman's outer garment was also longer than the man's; it covered the feet, and was fastened with a belt at the waist.

Headgear

Women wore squares of material on their heads, fastened with plaited cords. This helped protect them from the heat of the sun. Especially if they were unmarried, women often wore a veil over their faces out of modesty (Genesis 24:65).

Like the men, women often wore leather sandals. The strap went between the big toe and the second toe, and then round the heel (Luke 3:16).

Jewellery

Jewish women wore many pieces of jewellery, including bracelets on their wrists or above their elbows. They also wore bangles on their ankles, so that they jangled when they walked. The women often also wore earrings.

Jewish women used make-up, painting their eyelashes, and sometimes staining their fingers and toes red with a dye called henna (Isaiah 3:18-21).

Perfume

Women perfumed themselves with scents. They used scents such as frankincense and myrrh from Africa, aloes and nard from India, saffron from Palestine and many others.

Jewish women wore their hair long, and often arranged it in plaits.

Sandals

The poorest people often went barefoot. Others wore simple leather sandals, sometimes with wooden soles. Jesus' disciples wore sandals of this kind (see Mark 6:9). Jewish people took off their shoes when they entered a house. They had their feet washed before going inside.

Left: Costume of a Jewish woman;

above: costume of a rich woman. Notice her elaborate headgear and the bright colours of her clothes.

Tent life

When Abraham and his family first came to the Promised Land they lived in tents (Genesis 18:1-15). The tents of that time were quite simple. The Bedouin people live in similar tents in the desert today.

Building the tent
To build a tent, they first stuck wooden poles into the sand. Then they stretched a covering of cloth or animal skin, such as goat'shair, over the poles. They fixed down this covering by tying cords to it, and fastening the cords to tent-pegs hammered into the ground.

The tent covering became waterproof after rain had fallen on it and made it shrink. If the covering got torn, it could be mended by darning it.

Inside the tent
The ground inside the tent was covered with mats and carpets. Curtains divided off different parts of the tent. Cooking pots, food and family belongings were kept inside the tent, beside the tent-poles. The family would dig a little hole in the middle of the tent, and light a fire there to cook food on.

The tent door
The door was simply a flap of cloth that could be raised and lowered. No man was allowed inside the tent, except for the father of the family. Other men had to stay outside at the porch, which had a special cloth covering. If a stranger went inside the tent, he could be punished by being put to death (Judges 4:18, 21).

Furniture
Families living in tents had very little furniture. They were continually taking down the tent and moving on. They had to carry the tent poles and coverings with them on the backs of donkeys.

Tent people had straw mats to sit on, and used animal skins as tables. They kept water, milk and butter in bottles made from goatskins.

Right: The women of Bible times lived in a separate area of the tent, as Bedouin women do today.

Bedouin families still live in traditional style tents in the Judean Wilderness.

The House

The poorest people lived in very simple houses with only one room. This room could be as small as three metres (ten feet) square.

The house was usually built of mud bricks or of rough stones and rubble. Often insects and snakes lived in the loose walls (Amos 5:19). The walls were built very thick, to keep the house cool in the hot summer days, and warm during the cold winter nights.

Windows and door
There would be one little window, high up in the wall. It had no glass to keep out the wind and rain, but sometimes in winter the window was covered with an animal skin.

The house had a single small door, which was locked at night with a bar that was placed across it (Matthew 5:15). To light the room a little oil-lamp was placed on a shelf or on an upturned pot.

The lower area
There were usually two levels inside the house. The lower area, near the door, had a floor made of stamped-down earth. Often the family kept their animals, such as the donkey, sheep and guard-dog, in this section at night.

The family sometimes lit a fire in this part of the room, to warm the room and to cook their meals. Most houses had no chimney, so the walls and ceiling became black with soot, and the clouds of smoke set everyone coughing.

The upper area
The second level inside the house was a raised stone platform. On this platform the family would eat their meals, sit talking together and lie down to sleep at night. The family kept their food and pots on shelves or in little cupboards in the walls.

The roof
The house would have a flat roof made of wooden branches laid across thick wooden beams. After it

Interior of the house
The house was lit by an oil lamp. The flat roof was made of wooden branches laid across thick wooden beams. Notice the oil-lamp on the upturned pot.

rained, the roof had to be flattened down again with a roller; it was not very watertight. In spring, seeds that had blown onto the roof would start to sprout and make it look green.

The family made great use of the roof, which they reached by stairs up the outside wall of the house (2 Kings 19:26; Matthew 10:27; Acts 10:9). Often they dried grain and fruit on the roof, and stored part of the harvest there.

On hot summer nights, the family would take to the roof to sleep. Often the men would climb up onto the roof to pray, and they also stored their tools there. A special law said there had to be a low wall round the edge of the

roof to prevent people falling off (Deuteronomy 22:8).

During the day the family did not spend much time inside the house. They were busy working in the fields, or doing jobs in the courtyard or in the garden.

Furniture

Families usually had very little furniture. Most important was the chest in which they stored food or clothes. Often poor families turned the chest upside down and used it as a dining-table too. Some families had simple wooden stools or chairs to sit on, although many sat on the floor.

Poor people had only animal-skins to sleep on. Richer people had rough mattresses, and sometimes even wooden beds. For pillows, people used goatskins stuffed with wool or feathers.

Every family had an oil-lamp in the house. The cheaper lamps were made of clay; expensive ones were of bronze or other metals. These lamps burned olive oil, pitch or wax and had wicks made of flax. They were left to burn all through the night. The light showed anyone outside that there were people indoors sleeping. It was unheard of not to have a light.

Artist's impression of a peasant's house. Notice the low wall around the roof's edge, built for safety's sake.

Home life

Because they lived in a very hot country, most people got up before day-break so that they could do plenty of work before the sun got too hot. The mother would often get up before anyone else and light the fire, if it had gone out during the night.

After everyone had eaten breakfast, the men and the older boys would go off to the fields to work. The mother and the girls started their daily tasks. The young boys looked after the family's animals, such as the goat or the chickens, just as young Arab boys do today.

Milling

An important job was to grind the grain into flour to bake bread. Women ground the grain in a handmill made of two flat, round stones about fifty centimetres (eighteen inches) across. The bottom stone had a wooden peg in the centre; the top stone, which had a hole in the middle, fitted over this peg.

The woman would put handfuls of grain into the hole in the top stone. Then she slowly turned the handle on the top stone. As the two stones ground against each other, the grain was crushed between them. Fine flour poured onto the cloth that was laid beneath the two millstones. Often two women would do their milling together, to make it less hard work (Matthew 24:41).

Fetching water

Another daily job was fetching water for the family (Genesis 24:11-13). Often the older girls would do this. They would take goatskin bottles to a nearby spring or well and fill them with water. Then they would carefully carry them back, either balanced on their hips or on their shoulders. At the well they might meet other women on the same errand, and stop to chat.

There were plenty of other jobs to be done. The house had to be carefully swept and tidied. The area where the animals slept would particularly need cleaning out.

Baking bread

Each day there was also bread to be baked. This, too, was usually done by the women. They mixed the flour that they had milled with a little water. If the bread was to rise, they added a little dough from the previous day's bread, to act as yeast or 'leaven' (Matthew 13:33).

Then the dough was left to warm by the fire, so that the leaven could work its way through the dough. Finally the bread was ready to bake on the hot stones of a hearth.

Bread ovens

There were other ways of baking bread. Sometimes bread was baked on a big, shallow bowl that was turned upside down over the fire. The dough was rolled out very thin and laid over the top of the dish to bake. Another type of oven looked like an upside-down earthenware cone. A fire was lit at the bottom, and the dough was put inside to bake.

Washing clothes

Then there was the family's washing to be done. Sometimes this was done in a fast stream; sometimes by banging the dirt out of the wet clothes between flat stones. The women used soap made of olive oil or from a special vegetable.

Rest-time

At midday, when the sun was at its hottest, it was too uncomfortable to work. The family would find a shady place and take a couple of hours' rest. People in hot countries today still rest in the middle of the day.

Shopping

Although most families grew a lot of their own food, one or two extra things were usually needed for the evening meal. Some of the girls went to market most days to buy vegetables or meat.

Women ground the grain in a handmill made of two flat, round stones. Often two women would do their milling together, to make it less hard work.

Marriage

In Bible times, young people did not normally decide for themselves who to marry. Their parents usually chose for them.

The bride's price
Once a wife had been chosen for a son, there were money arrangements to be made. The bride's mother and father had to be paid for losing their daughter. Also, the bride's father gave his daughter a special gift of money, called a dowry (Genesis 24:59-61).

Betrothal
Once all the arrangements had been made, the man and woman were bound by vows, or 'betrothed', to be married (Matthew 1:18-20). The time of betrothal lasted a year, while everyone prepared for the wedding itself. The bride's family made her wedding clothes and arranged the wedding feast.

The wedding
At the wedding, the bride and groom made a legal agreement and a blessing was said over them. Then came the wedding feast, when everyone dressed in their special wedding clothes. The feast was usually given by the bride's family.

A bride wearing her traditional headdress.

The procession
On the marriage day, there was a special procession. The bridegroom, dressed in his best clothes and decorated with jewels, walked with his friends from his home to his bride's home. She would be waiting, having dressed after being bathed by her bridesmaids (Psalm 45:14-15). She wore a veil to cover her face.

The feast
Once the groom arrived, everyone walked back to his house, the guests holding oil lamps to light the way. When they entered the bridegroom's house, the bride and groom sat down under a special canopy and the feast began.

Feasting could last as long as seven days (Judges 14:12), with much drinking, eating, dancing and singing. Jesus once went to a wedding at the village of Cana, near his home town of Nazareth (see John 2).

Children

Jewish parents believed it was a sign of God's blessing if they had many children (Deuteronomy 28:4). The more children the better, especially if they were boys. If a woman was childless, people made fun of her, or pitied her.

Birth
When a pregnant woman was ready to give birth, the midwife would be called to her house (Exodus 1:15-19). Birth took place at home; there were no hospitals as we know them.

The newborn baby was first washed, and then rubbed down with salt, water and oil. People thought this was good for the baby's skin. After this, the baby was wrapped up very tightly with strips of bandage. People believed this would help the baby's legs and arms grow straight.

When a male child was eight days old, there was a special ceremony, called circumcision. The loose skin on his penis was cut off, as a sign that the boy was being given back to God (Genesis 17:10).

Names
At about the same time, the baby was named (Luke 2:21). Names were very important, and each name had its own meaning. For example, David means 'beloved', and Sarah means 'princess'.

Childhood
As soon as children were old enough, they were expected to help with household chores. There was sweeping to be done, water to be fetched and animals to be looked after.

From about the age of three, the father began to teach his son the stories of God's law. Later he started to train him in his own craft or trade. Joseph taught his son Jesus his craft as a carpenter.

Children were taught to ask questions about their nation's past. 'In time to come your children will ask you, "Why did the LORD our God command us to obey all these laws?"' (Deuteronomy 6:20-25).

School
Jesus went to school

Until the time of Jesus, there were no schools. A child's parents taught him or her everything they knew. The children were told about the religious festivals, such as Passover, and what they meant.

By the time of Jesus, boys of six and over went to school at the 'house of the book'. The teacher was paid by the synagogue, the Jewish meeting-place. The boys would learn by heart passages from Scripture, and be taught to read and write.

Classes
School lasted only about four hours each day. After morning class there was a long break until afternoon class started, at about three o'clock. But classes went on all the year round – there were no school holidays.

The teacher sat cross-legged on a little platform in front of the class. Before him was a little rack where he kept scrolls containing parts of the Scripture. The boys sat on the floor in front of their teacher. All the boys were in one class, whatever age they were.

The boys wrote on wooden tablets covered with a thin layer of wax, using pointed sticks to make marks in the wax (Luke 1:63).

Growing up
13 yrs = man

When a boy reached the age of thirteen he was regarded as a man. There was a special ceremony to mark this stage in his life. When he was twelve, Jesus went to the Temple in Jerusalem with his parents for his last Passover as a child (see Luke 2:41-49). Jewish boys today have a ceremony called the Barmitzvah when they are about thirteen. Afterwards they can go as adults to the synagogue.

Toys and games
Children didn't have many toys to play with. They usually made do with sticks or bits of string and broken pottery. Some children had toys made out of clay, and some girls had clay dolls dressed in rag dresses.

Jesus talks about children playing games in the streets – they sound like dance games (see Matthew 11:16-17.

Health and Medicine

The Jews had many special rules to make sure they led healthy lives. They were to keep one day in seven as a day of rest. They were not to eat certain unhealthy foods. They were to make sure that their food and their homes were clean.

The Jews believed they should pray to God when they were ill. But sometimes they copied surrounding nations, by wearing lucky charms to keep away evil spirits.

Medicines

The Jews gradually began to use simple natural drugs. They knew how to clean wounds and bandage them, using natural ointments for cuts. They used a herb called myrrh mixed with wine as a pain-killer. *myrrh*

Diseases

We know from stories in the Bible that people suffered from many different illnesses and diseases, such as leprosy, blindness, deafness, epilepsy and as cripples (Mark 1:32-34). Many Jews believed that illness came as a result of their sins. If someone was ill, they would ask: 'Was this person a sinner – or his mother or father?' (John 9:2-4).

Doctors

In Jesus' time some doctors were trained by the Greeks to do surgical operations. They took vows promising to put the life of their patient first, and not to give away personal details about their patients.

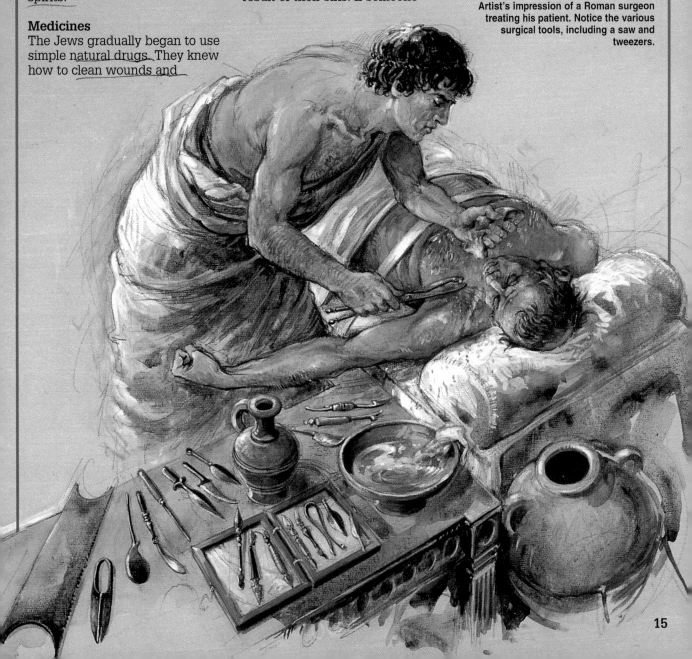

Artist's impression of a Roman surgeon treating his patient. Notice the various surgical tools, including a saw and tweezers.

15

Growing Grain

wheat & barley millet

Farmers in Bible times grew mainly wheat and barley, and sometimes a grain called millet. Barley could be grown on poorer land, but it was not so popular as wheat.

Sowing seed

The farmer scattered seed from a basket. As he sowed, he ploughed the seed into the soil, to stop the birds flying off with it. Jesus describes a sower at work in Luke 8:5-8.

While the grain was growing, from December to February, the farmer had to weed the land so that the grain was not choked by weeds.

Harvest

Barley was ready to harvest in April or May. The farmer cut it

A farmer harvests the grain with his sickle.

down, using a sharp curved tool called a sickle (Jeremiah 50:16). He cut the barley stalks near the top, and left the rest of the plant in the ground, so that his sheep could graze there afterwards.

The farmer left some grain standing in the corners of his fields. Poor people were allowed to come and take this grain, or any other grain that the farmer and his workers had missed (Ruth 2).

Threshing

Now the grain had to be separated from the straw stems. The grain was taken to a patch of hard ground (1 Chronicles 21:18-26). Here it was beaten with sticks or trampled by oxen to separate it.

Sometimes the farmer used a threshing board. This was a wooden board with stones or iron spikes fixed underneath. Oxen pulled it over the grain, to thresh it.

Ploughing

The farmer started off by ploughing up his land in October or November, when the rain came (Matthew 13:4). The rain helped soften the parched earth, and made it easier to plough. Often the farmer ploughed and sowed his seed at the same time. The plough was a T-shaped wooden tool with a sharp spike that cut through the soil. It was drawn by two donkeys or two oxen. If the field was on a hill or near trees, the farmer had to break up the soil by hand. To do this he used a tool like a hoe, called a mattock (Isaiah 7:25).

farmers

Winnowing

After the threshing, the farmer had to separate the grain from the chaff – the bits of straw and the outer husk. He did this by tossing the grain in the air, using a wooden winnowing fork. The chaff was light and was blown away on the wind; but the grain was heavier and fell to the ground.

Finally the farmer shook his grain in a big sieve to get rid of any bits of waste or weeds (Luke 22:31).

Storage

Now the farmer could store his precious grain. He usually put his grain in great earthenware pots or jars (Luke 6:38).

Harvest was a very important time. It provided the grain for another year's bread. So the people celebrated the barley harvest and the wheat harvest each year with special feasts (*see* page 31)..

Eating and Drinking

Breakfast
Breakfast, the first meal of the day, was not a big meal. The family would usually eat bread and cheese and some fruit or olives. The men might take their breakfast with them to the fields.

Evening meal
The main meal of the day was in the evening, when work was finished and the sun was less hot. The women prepared a pot of vegetable stew or lentils (Genesis 25:29, 34), which was simmering over the fire when the men returned from the fields.

Everyone would scoop food out of the pot, using a piece of bread. There were no knives and forks to eat with. They might drink wine with the meal, and on special occasions they might have some meat too. They often finished the meal with fruit.

Feasts
The Jewish people enjoyed having special feasts. They held feasts when people got married, on birthdays, at burials and at sheep-shearing time. They also ate well if there were guests to entertain. There were special religious festivals too – such as Passover, Purim and Harvest (see page 31).

At the festivals, they often added meat to the usual stew. Also, they might have special sweet pastries with the fruit. The feasts were very happy times, with plenty of singing and dancing. Wedding feasts lasted for days (see page 12), as they still do in many Arab villages.

Food

Bread
Bread, the basic food, was eaten at every meal. Jesus taught his followers to pray: 'Give us each day our daily bread' (Luke 11:3).

Barley stew with lentils.

The Jewish people didn't use knives to cut slices of bread; they used their bare hands to tear off pieces to eat.

Milk
The Jews drank the milk of sheep, and of goats and camels too. They used milk to make cheese and butter (2 Samuel 17:29). They also made a kind of yogurt by shaking milk in a skin bag (Genesis 18:8). The Bedouin people today make yogurt in a similar way.

Vegetables
The Jewish people grew and ate several different vegetables. They had plenty of beans, lentils, gherkins and cucumbers for their stews (Ezekiel 4:9). They also had root vegetables, and herbs to flavour their stews.

Fruit and nuts
The Jews ate plenty of fruit. Many different fruit grow well in the warm climate of Israel. When Moses sent spies to explore the Promised Land, they brought back huge bunches of grapes to show how rich the land was.

As well as grapes, the country was rich in pomegranates, figs, dates, olives, almonds and pistachio nuts (Jeremiah 24:2; Genesis 43:11; Deuteronomy 8:8).

Honey
The Jews obtained honey from wild bees (Judges 14:8-9). Honey was important as a sweetener, because they had no sugar. Another sort of honey was made by boiling grape juice down until it was syrupy and sweet. They often spread this syrup on bread to eat.

Meat
Most families did not normally eat meat. They usually only tasted meat at special feasts (1 Kings 4:23). The Jews sometimes ate birds such as pigeons, geese, quails and partridge. The most common meat was the kid, or young goat, but they also ate lamb.

Fish
Fish from the Sea of Galilee and from the River Jordan was a favourite food (Luke 11:11). In the time of Jesus many fishermen sailed on Galilee to bring in fish.

Wine
For most people the main drink was wine. Much of the grape juice was used to make wine. Water was often dirty and full of germs, so it was safer to drink wine.

Olives and Grapes

Almost every family had olive trees, often growing in little groves. Olive trees grow well in dry lands like Palestine. They have very deep roots and can find water deep in the earth. It is about fifteen years before an olive tree starts to bear fruit; but it can live many years longer than this.

Olive harvest
The olives were ready to pick in September and October. They were gathered in a cloth laid out under the tree. Boys would beat and shake the tree, and the ripe olives would drop into the cloth below. Some of the olives were eaten raw, and others were preserved in salted water. But most of the olives were crushed to make olive oil.

The olive press
The olives were crushed in a special olive press. This was made up of a big stone with a hollow on top where the olives were placed for crushing. A stone wheel placed over the olives was turned, pressing the oil out of them. The oil was collected in jars and stored for use.

Olive oil
Olive oil had many uses. It was used instead of butter on bread, and as cooking fat. It was also used to burn in lamps (Matthew 25:3,4), and to make soap. Olive oil was also rubbed into the skin to make it shine, and as an ointment for wounds.

Planting grapes
The grape harvest was nearly as important as the grain harvest. Grape vines were best planted on a hillside (Isaiah 5:1). The grapes would catch the sun well there, and the rain would run off the slope. Often the hillside would be stepped into a series of little terraces running along the slope. The edge of each terrace was marked with a little wall of stones and rocks.

Before planting new vines, the farmer broke up the soil with his hoe or mattock. Then he planted out the vines, leaving plenty of room between them. While some vines grew along the ground, others needed sticks to climb on.

Pruning
During the winter the farmer cut out dead or broken branches. This left the healthy branches to grow and bear grapes. Jesus talked about pruning grapes (see John 15:1-6).

Grape harvest
When the grapes were ready to pick, in July, August or September, the farmer's family often went to live in a watch-tower among the vines (Isaiah 5:2). At night they could guard the grapes from thieves, and during the day they picked the grapes, collecting them in big baskets.

The grape harvest was a festival time (see page 31). There was much singing and dancing as well as plenty of hard work.

Using the grapes
Some of the grapes were eaten fresh. Some grapes were crushed to make fresh grape-juice. Yet other grapes were spread out to dry in the sun to make raisins.

But most of the grapes were pressed to make wine. These grapes were put into a square tank cut into the rock. People would tread the grapes to press out the juice. As it ran out, the juice was collected in a pot or jar. Everyone enjoyed treading the grapes!

Storage
The juice was left for about six months to ferment into wine. Then it was poured into storage jars, carefully leaving behind the waste that had sunk to the bottom (Jeremiah 48:11). Sometimes wine was stored in goatskin bottles instead of jars.

The Shepherd

Shepherds at Jesus' birth

Sheep were much valued in Bible times. They provided wool, meat and milk. Even the sheep's horns were used – to make special trumpets (Leviticus 25:9) or as containers for oil.

Sheep and goats
In Bible times, the shepherd looked after the goats and sheep together in the same flock. Goats gave a lot of milk, and some of it was used to make a kind of yogurt. Goat'shair was used to make a coarse cloth used for covering tents and for rough clothes, while goatskin leather was used to make water bottles.

The shepherd often looked after the sheep and goats belonging to everyone in his village. After the rain had fallen in winter, there was plenty of grass near the village for the flocks and herds to graze on, and when the grain had been cut at harvest, the sheep and goats grazed on the stubble left behind.

New pasture
But when the hot summer sun had dried the grass, the shepherd had to lead the flocks further away to find pasture (1 Chronicles 4:39-40). He also had to find a well where he could draw water for the sheep and goats to drink.

The shepherd also had to guard his flock from the wild animals that roamed the country (1 Samuel 17:34-36). Lions, bears, jackals and hyena were all looking for animals such as sheep to eat.

Shepherds' tools
The shepherd carried a heavy club spiked with sharp stones to beat off animals (Psalm 23:4). He also had a leather sling for throwing stones at wild animals.

The shepherd had a staff about two metres (six feet) long. He used this as a walking stick in rough country, and to control his sheep (Ezekiel 20:37-38). Sometimes his rod had a hook, or crook, at one end.

The shepherd also had a leather bag, called a scrip, to carry his food. Some shepherds had a little reed pipe to play while they were watching the sheep and goats.

Shelter
At night the shepherd had to find a safe place to shelter his sheep (Luke 2:8). Often he would take his sheep to a cave, and sleep in the doorway to prevent wild animals from entering (John 10:7). Sometimes, if there was no cave, he had to make a rough stockade out of stones or brushwood.

In the village, there would sometimes be a stone sheepfold, with a little shelter for the guarding shepherd.

An Eastern shepherd tends his flock. For such men, little has changed since biblical times.

The shepherd spent a lot of time alone with his sheep, and learned to know them all by name (John 10:14). He knew which sheep belonged to which family, and could return them to their owners.

Sheep-shearing
At the end of summer the sheep would be sheared. When sheep-shearing was finished, they celebrated with a feast, and plenty of eating and drinking (1 Samuel 25).

Jesus described a shepherd looking for his lost sheep in Luke 15: 3-7. There is also a fine description of the shepherd's job in Psalm 23.

Fishing

In Jesus' time, many fishermen worked on the big lake called the Sea of Galilee, and many fishing villages surrounded the lake. Some of these fishermen used a rod and line, like anglers today.

Cast net

Some fishermen used a cast net (Mark 1:16-17). This was a circular net, about five metres (17 feet) across. It had weights tied round the edge, and a rope tied to the middle. When a fisherman could see fish in shallow water by the water's edge, he would wade into the water and drop the net over them. The weights pulled the net down, trapping the fish.

Seine net

If they were fishing from a boat, fishermen would often use a seine net (Luke 5:4). This was a long net, about three metres (10 feet) wide, that was let out behind the boat. It had corks fixed to the top to make it float, and stones tied to the bottom to weigh it down.

Fish were caught in the net as the boat sailed along. Sometimes the boat turned in a circle so that the fish were caught in the middle of the net.

Fishing boats

The fishermen used small sailing boats that normally held only about four men. These boats had one big sail, and a long oar to steer with.

When they had finished a day's fishing, the men would lay out their nets to dry, and mend any tears in them.

Craft workers

Tinkmaker

The Potter

In Bible times, clay was used to make pots for eating and drinking from, and for storing things. This clay was dug from the ground, and it had to be mixed with water to make it soft enough to shape.

Coil pots

The first potters made bowls and jugs by rolling out long snakes of clay and then coiling them up. Then they smoothed out the bumpy surface and left the pot to dry hard.

Later, potters found they could make smooth, round pots by using a special wheel. They put the clay on a flat, turning wheel. This wheel was often turned by another worker. Then potters learned to turn it by pushing their feet on a second wheel attached below (Ecclesiasticus 38:29).

Decorating the pots

Once the pots had dried, they were often decorated. Sometimes

red or black was added to make a pattern, or the clay was smoothed to give it a shiny surface.

The potter's mould

If he wanted to make complicated shapes, the potter could not use his wheel. Oil lamps, which had a lip on one side, were made by pressing clay into a wooden mould to shape it. The potter also made some things by hand, such as toys, ornaments and little figures.

Firing the clay

Once the clay had dried, the potter put it in a special oven to 'fire' it. The clay pots would come out hard enough to use, but they broke very easily if they were knocked.

The Leatherworker

Leather was used to make many different things, such as bottles, belts, soldiers' helmets, shields and slings.

Skinning the animal

First the leatherworker had to prepare his leather. He would skin a goat or ox to get its hide (skin). Then he scraped the skin to remove all the animal's hair. Finally, he soaked the skin and put lime on it, to remove any remaining hair.

Softening the skin

Next the leatherworker softened the leather by soaking it in water with special leaves in it, by rubbing it with dog droppings and by hammering it. His workshop could smell very bad!

Leather goods

Sometimes the tanner, or leatherworker, dyed the leather, before starting to make sandals, belts or other articles to sell.

Sandals

The carpenter

The carpenter had two jobs – building houses and making furniture. Carpenters had to be tough, strong men.

Building a house

To build a house, the carpenter had to cut down trees. Then he shaped the logs he had cut to use as beams for the roof. He used tools such as a handsaw and an axe to do this work. The axe head was made of stone or bronze and was lashed to a wooden handle.

Making furniture

But the carpenter did many smaller jobs too. He made doors and doorframes, wooden locks, tables, stools and chests for the home. He also made ploughs, yokes and shovels for the farmer.

Working with cloth

The Jewish people made many of their clothes from sheep's wool.

Spinning

Before the wool could be spun, the women had to wash and comb it. Then they spun the wool into lengths on a special wooden stick.

Dyeing

After this the women washed the wool again before dyeing it (Jeremiah 2:22). The dyes they used were made of crushed shells (Acts 16:14), fruit, or even lice eggs, and were mixed with water. The wool was dyed in big pots or basins, then rinsed in water and dried.

An Eastern woman weaves at an outdoor loom.

Weaving

Once the wool had been spun and dyed, it was ready to be woven into cloth. Often the loom was set up outdoors, on a simple wooden frame (Judges 16:13).

First the weaver would fix the long warp threads from end to end. Then she would push the yarn between the warp threads, using a wooden stick to guide it through. Gradually a piece of cloth would be formed, as the weft, or cross-, threads grew.

Boy who ran away naked in Gospel
Might have had inner clothing on.

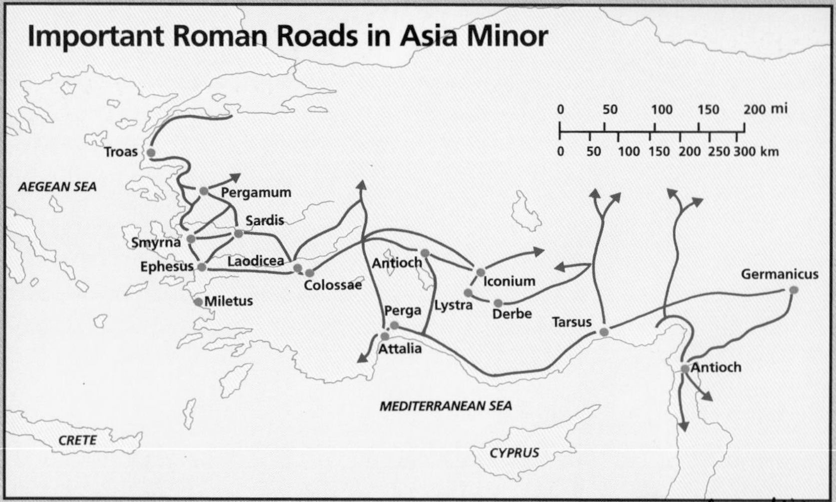

Important Roman Roads in Asia Minor

[Map showing Roman roads in Asia Minor with locations labeled:]
Troas, Pergamum, Sardis, Smyrna, Ephesus, Laodicea, Miletus, Colossae, Antioch, Perga, Lystra, Derbe, Iconium, Attalia, Tarsus, Germanicus, Antioch

AEGEAN SEA, MEDITERRANEAN SEA, CRETE, CYPRUS

Scale: 0 50 100 150 200 mi / 0 50 100 150 200 250 300 km

Some rich Romans were carried in special chairs by their slaves.

Travel

In Bible times there were no railways, planes or cars to take people from place to place. Because travel was so difficult and dangerous (2 Corinthians 11:26-27), people only left home if they had to. Most people travelled on foot, while those who could afford it went on horseback or by horse-drawn carriage.

Difficult country
Palestine is a bare, hilly country. It is difficult for travel, and there were few good roads in Bible times. The best roads were built by the Romans. Their roads were straight and level. They enabled the Roman army to march rapidly if trouble arose.

[handwritten annotation: 16-20 Rom. Miles]

Most people could walk sixteen to twenty Roman miles in a day. We know from the Gospels that Jesus and his followers travelled on foot around Galilee. The book of Acts tells how the apostle Paul walked long distances through what we know as Turkey and Greece, taking the good news about Jesus.

Danger, thief!
The roads were often dangerous, with thieves lying in wait for travellers. Jesus told a story about a traveller who was set upon by thieves (Luke 10:30-35). In his story, the Samaritan who found the wounded traveller took him to a roadside inn. There were many inns like this, where a traveller could find food and a bed for the night.

Chariots and carts
Sometimes farmers or merchants used carts drawn by oxen or by horses to carry grain and other goods. Some rich people could afford to travel in horse-drawn carriages (Acts 8:29).

Pack animals
Poorer people used a donkey or mule to carry their heavy loads, tying sacks onto the animal's back (Genesis 42:25-28). They also used donkeys to turn mill-wheels and water-wheels.

The camel
The camel can store enough water to last several days, making it an ideal creature for travelling in hot deserts. In Bible times the camel was often used by merchants crossing the desert with their goods (Judges 6:5).

Mule

Horse-drawn carriage

Military chariot

Military horseman

Sea travel

The Jews didn't often travel by sea, because they thought it was very dangerous. Palestine is on the Mediterranean Sea, where it was unsafe to sail in winter because wild storms can arise.

In Jesus' time, the Romans sailed big ships to the ports of Palestine. They used them to carry soldiers, grain and other goods. We know that the apostle Paul sailed to Rome in a grain ship that held 276 people, similar to the ship illustrated below (Acts 27:6). These ships only had one sail on a single mast, and were difficult to handle in stormy weather.

Horse-drawn carriage

Replica of a Roman siege engine and catapult (*background*) near Masada, Israel.

Chariots

Some armies had horse-drawn chariots. The chariots were mainly used to carry archers, so that they could fire their arrows freely at the enemy. Sometimes their arrows had special spikes, or barbs, to prevent their being easily pulled out of a wound.

Siege

Often enemy armies surrounded a town and set up a siege. Cities were built with high walls around them to protect them from enemies. An attacking army would try to tunnel beneath the walls, or knock a hole by using a battering-ram. The Romans also used giant catapults that threw great rocks into a city.

The people inside a besieged city would throw stones or boiling oil at the soldiers outside, to stop them getting in.

The Roman army

The Roman army controlled Palestine in Jesus' time. They were very well organised and equipped; each soldier had armour consisting of a breastplate, helmet and shield (Ephesians 6:13-17). He also had a full set of weapons: a dagger, long sword and javelin. The Romans also trained specialist soldiers such as bowmen, horsemen, surgeons and engineers.

Weapons and War

The Jews were surrounded by enemy nations, but it was not until the time of King Solomon that they could afford to have a regular army. Solomon raised taxes to pay for his army, and built new strongholds to guard the roads.

Weapons

However the Jewish soldiers were often poorly armed. Enemy armies such as the Assyrians had fine coats of mail, and metal shields and helmets, whereas the Jewish soldiers often had only a simple weapon such as a sling. Shields usually consisted of a wooden frame covered with leather. Foot soldiers had a dagger and a throwing spear (1 Samuel 18:10-11), while some soldiers were specially trained to use slings or bows and arrows.

Egyptian warrior.　　Philistine warrior.　　Assyrian spearman.　　Babylonian spearman.　　Greek soldier.　　Israelite archer.

A Roman centurion (foreground) and Roman legionary soldier (background). The legionary is armed with a long sword, a short sword and a javelin, and has a large shield for protection. The centurion commanded a force of one hundred soldiers.

Religion and Festivals

Sabbath
The Jews worked very hard for most of the week, but they believed that God wanted them to rest on one day in seven (Exodus 20:8-11). Their day of rest was called the 'Sabbath'.

In Jesus' time, people went to the synagogue to worship on the Sabbath, and then came home for a good meal.

The synagogue
The synagogue was their religious meeting-place. The men entered through the main door and sat together. The women had a separate door leading to stairs to the gallery, where they sat with the children.

Inside the synagogue was a special cupboard where the scrolls containing the Scriptures were kept. In the centre stood a pulpit with a reading-desk, from which men preached and read aloud the Scriptures (Luke 4:16-21). During services, the men also sang psalms.

Festivals

The people celebrated many special festivals during the year. They had festivals to give thanks for the barley harvest, wheat harvest and grape harvest. At each of these harvest festivals the Jews also remembered a great religious event in their past.

Passover/Barley Harvest

At the barley harvest festival, which lasted a whole week, the people remembered the time when God had helped them escape from captivity in Egypt. This festival, called *Pessach* in Hebrew, took place in spring.

Each family had a special meal together, called *Seder*, to remind them of leaving Egypt. The youngest boy in the family would ask the oldest man questions about that time. They ate bread without yeast, to remind them of the bread that was cooked in a hurry before the Israelites left Egypt (Exodus 12:7; 13:3-10), and bitter herbs, to remind them of the bitterness of slavery in Egypt. They drank red wine to show their thanks to God.

Pentecost/Wheat Harvest

This festival came in the middle of the wheat harvest. A little field was harvested, and the wheat from it used to make two special loaves. The people waved the loaves in the air to thank God for the harvest (Leviticus 23:15-21). At this festival, the Jews specially remembered the time when Moses received the Ten Commandments at Mount Sinai (see Exodus 20).

Tents/Grape Harvest

This festival lasted a whole week and came when all the grapes had been harvested. To remind them that the Israelites had lived in tents during their long journey from Egypt to the Promised Land (Leviticus 23), families built special tent-like shelters out of branches and palm leaves, and lived in them for the week. In the capital, Jerusalem, great candlesticks were lit in the temple, and flaming torches burned throughout the city.

An artist's impression of Herod's Temple, Jerusalem. This magnificent building was the focus of Jewish worship; here the priests made daily sacrifices, and the priests and high priest celebrated the great yearly festivals.

Other Festivals

Festival of Trumpets

On this day, which marked the start of the New Year, priests blew special ram's-horn trumpets (Numbers 10:10).

The Day of Atonement

Known in Hebrew as *Yom Kippur* (Leviticus 16), this was the most solemn day of the year for the Jews. On this day, the High Priest entered the Holiest Place in the Temple in Jerusalem, dressed in white. Then he sprinkled the blood of a goat and a bull that had been sacrificed, showing that God accepted the people's sacrifices.

Purim

This was a festival of rejoicing. The Jews remembered the time when Queen Esther had saved her people from being wiped out by the king of Persia. The Jews today still mark this festival with fun and rejoicing (Esther).

Lights

This festival, known as *Channukah* in Hebrew, marked the time when the Jews drove the Syrians out of Jerusalem and re-dedicated the Temple to the worship of God (2 Maccabees 10:6). As at the festival of Tents, there were special lights in the Temple, and each family lit a special candle.

Death and Burial

In Bible times, many people died before old age. They died through illness, poverty or famine.

When someone died

As soon as someone died, friends and relatives began to wail and lament. This let neighbours know somebody had died. The family would come together to wail.

Sometimes rich families would pay for other people to come and wail for them (Jeremiah 9:17-18). While they were in mourning, people often wore rough goat'shair clothes, sometimes called sackcloth. Or they tore their clothes, to show how sad they were.

Burial

Because the weather was often very hot, it was important to bury the dead before the body started to rot. Usually the body was washed and wrapped up in linen before being carried on a stretcher to the burying place.

People were often buried in caves, or in specially dug-out tombs in the rock (Judges 8:32). But there were not enough caves for all the bodies. So, when bodies had rotted away, the bones were collected and saved in special bone-boxes (called ossuaries) to make room in the caves for new bodies.

Burial caves

These burial caves were closed up with huge rocks. Sometimes the door was a circular stone that rolled across the opening in a slot (see Luke 24:1-2).

Poorer people were sometimes buried more simply (Luke 7:14). The stretcher with the body was laid on the ground, covered with earth and surrounded by rocks.

A stone-cut tomb of Bible times, guarded by a great circular stone across its entrance.

Index